ASTROLOGY

EMBROIDERY

Maya Hanisch

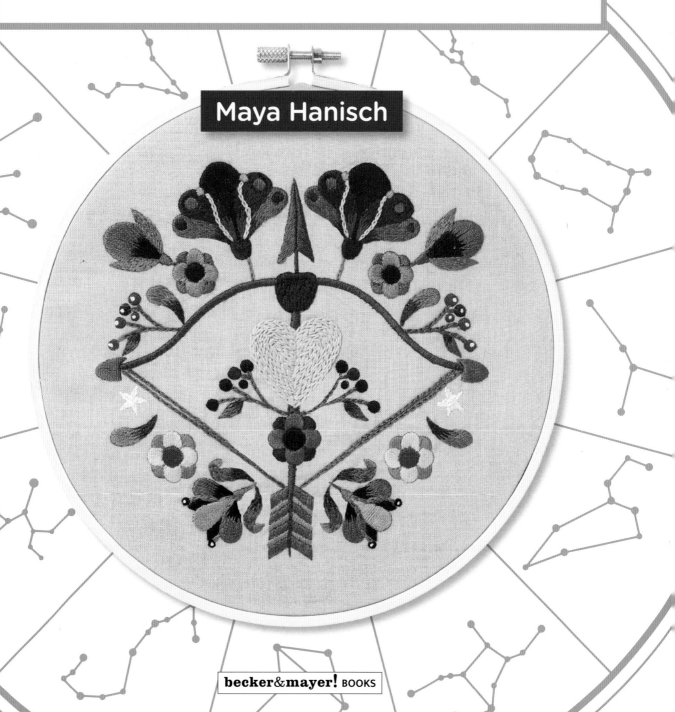

becker&mayer! BOOKS

Brimming with creative inspiration, how-to projects, and useful information to enrich your everyday life, Quarto Knows is a favorite destination for those pursuing their interests and passions. Visit our site and dig deeper with our books into your area of interest: Quarto Creates, Quarto Cooks, Quarto Homes, Quarto Lives, Quarto Drives, Quarto Explores, Quarto Gifts, or Quarto Kids.

© 2021 Quarto Publishing Group USA Inc.

Published in 2021 by becker&mayer! books, an imprint of The Quarto Group, 11120 NE 33rd Place, Suite 201, Bellevue, WA 98004 USA.

www.QuartoKnows.com

becker&mayer! books titles are also available at discount for retail, wholesale, promotional, and bulk purchase. For details, contact the Special Sales Manager by email at specialsales@quarto.com or by mail at The Quarto Group, Attn: Special Sales Manager, 100 Cummings Center Suite 265D, Beverly, MA 01915 USA.

21 22 23 24 25   5 4 3 2 1

ISBN: 978-0-7603-7225-8

Library of Congress Cataloging-in-Publication Data available upon request.

Author and illustrator: Maya Hanisch
Photographs by Chris Burrows

Printed, manufactured, and assembled in Guongdong, China

Image credits: Shutterstock

#346050

CONTENTS

THE ZODIAC

MORE CELESTIAL PATTERNS

ZODIAC CONSTELLATIONS

INTRODUCTION

Through the centuries, people have looked to the night sky for inspiration and guidance. Western astrology holds that the stars provide insight into our lives and in today's changing world looking to the ever-steady stars is more appealing than ever.

Hand embroidery offers a different sort of relief in turbulent times. Taking a moment to unplug and focus on the simple rhythm of stitching colorful images in cloth can have a calming, meditative effect. This book marries these two sources of calm and clarity.

My designs are inspired by folkloric patterns, present in the ancient costumes and arts of various cultures in the world. Symmetries of animals, flowers and different elements of nature in a composition that dances hand in hand with every zodiac sign.

While you stitch these design I hope you take time to reflect on the wonders and wisdom of the galaxy as you stitch the stars in your embroidery hoop.

Maya

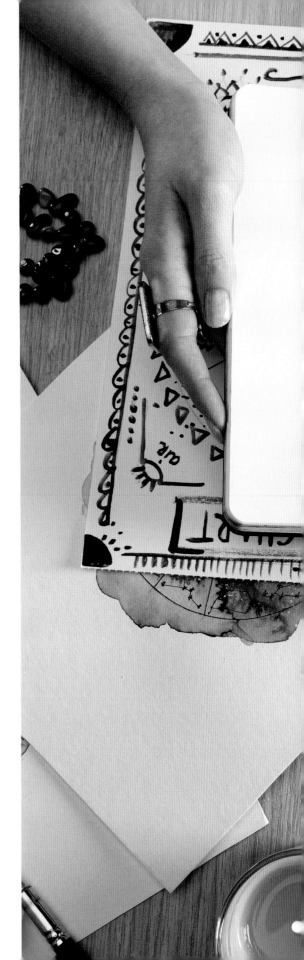

TOOLS & MATERIALS

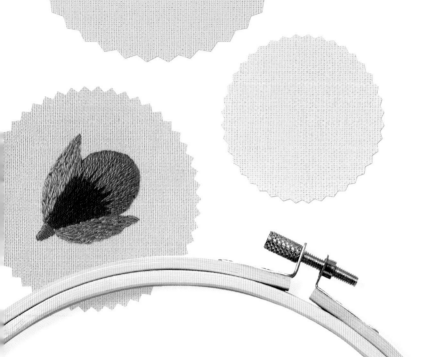

FABRIC

When choosing fabric, look for a smooth cotton or linen that has a tight weave and isn't too thick.

Backing your embroidery fabric is optional, but tacking a piece of cotton voile or finely woven muslin fabric to the back helps stabilize your stitching and gives you the option of starting (and ending) new threads with a small double stitch through the backing fabric only.

HOOP

An embroidery hoop helps keeps your fabric taut and stops your work from puckering as you stitch.

Place the inner hoop on a flat surface and lay your fabric over the top with the section of the design you're about to embroider in the center. Loosen the screw on the outer hoop just enough so it slips over the fabric and sandwiches it between the inner and outer hoops, then tighten the screw.

Grip your fabric on either side of the hoop and pull it taut (you want it drum tight), but take care not to distort the design when you do this. You may need to redo this last step a few times as you embroider, as the fabric might sag a bit in the hoop after stitching for a while. Move your hoop around so you're able to work the stitches comfortably.

NEEDLES

Embroidery needle

Sometimes called crewel needles, embroidery needles have a long, oval eye that can hold numerous strands of thread. They come in various sizes and your thread should pull easily through the eye, but not so much so that it slips out while you're stitching.

Milliners needle

Sometimes called a straw needle, these needles are the same width from eye to tip and are suited to doing French and bullion knots as they pull easily through wraps of thread.

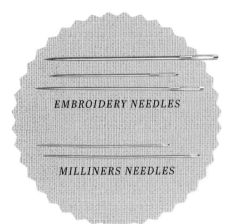

EMBROIDERY NEEDLES

MILLINERS NEEDLES

Each project uses 6-stranded, cotton DMC embroidery floss. DMC is one of the largest brands of vembroidery floss and it is available at most craft and fabric stores. The colors listed in each pattern are labeled with a corresponding DMC color code number.

THREADS

Cotton embroidery threads are made up of six strands twisted into one piece of thread, which you can split up into strands as needed. Cut a piece of thread about 16 inches (40 cm) long and divide it into the number of strands you need at one end, then slide a finger between the strands and down the length of the thread to separate them.

Certain stitches turn out better when the individual strands have been split apart and regrouped before use. These include back, satin, and straight stitches. For stitches such as stem, chain, and others where the individual strands aren't as visible, separating your thread into individual strands isn't always necessary.

When your stitches start looking thin and scraggly, your thread is likely stripped or it has become too tightly twisted. If stripped, end off and start a new piece of thread. If too tightly wound, spin your needle between your thumb and forefinger to untwist it or turn your hoop upside down and let your needle dangle until the thread has untwisted itself.

USING EMBROIDERY FLOSS:

The six strands in each skein of floss are designed to be separated. For the thinnest lines and knots used only 1 strand. Increase to 2 or 3 strands when creating thicker lines. After you cut a length of floss, separate two strands from the rest, then thread your needle. Set the remaining strands aside for later use.

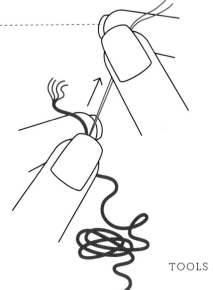

PATTERN TRANSFER TECHNIQUES

There are many ways to transfer printed patterns onto your fabric. Below are some of them.

Iron-On Transfers

Iron-on transfers are printed using special ink that allows you to transfer designs onto fabric accurately using a hot iron. To use this technique, digitally scan the design from the back of the book and print it onto iron-on transfer sheets. The designs are reversed so they will appear in the right direction on the fabric once transferred. Each design printed onto the transfer sheet should transfer onto fabric multiple times before it fades. The longer you iron, the darker and thicker the lines will be and the fewer transfers you'll get out of each design. The ink may fade with washing, but this is not guaranteed, so be sure to embroider over all the lines.

Cut it out from the transfer sheet and place it face-down on your fabric. Press the back firmly with a hot, dry iron for 5-to-10 seconds. You can slide the iron gently over the design if necessary, but make sure it doesn't move and transfer double lines. Raise a corner of the transfer paper to check that the design has transferred properly before lifting it off the fabric.

Other Transfer Techniques

A water-soluble pen is a simple way to transfer a design. Make a photocopy of the motif and tape it to a window, which will act as a light box. Tape your fabric over the design and trace with the water-soluble pen.

For fabrics that are too dark or thick to use the window/light box method, you can use water-soluble fabric stabilizer. Using carbon paper, trace the design onto the stabilizer. Adhere the stabilizer to the front of the fabric. After you have placed your fabric and stabilizer in the hoop, you will stitch through the fabric and stabilizer together and then remove the stabilizer according to the package directions.

STITCH GUIDE

HOW TO START AND END THREADS

To prevent your embroidery stitches from coming undone, you need to secure the start and end of each thread. Ways of doing this depend on personal preference and the stitch you intend to use. For example, use a knot when the lump it may make underneath the fabric won't be visible—like when embroidering French knots. Finish off each thread as you finish stitching to secure it, and cut off any excess so it won't get tangled in your working thread.

DOUBLE STITCH

If you're using backing fabric, only make a small double stitch through the backing fabric underneath the section you're about to embroider. Then bring the thread to the front and begin stitching. Cut off any excess thread.

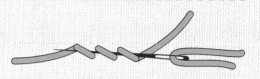

KNOT

Hold the tail end of your thread as well as the eye end of the needle between your thumb and forefinger and wrap the thread around the needle two or three times. Holding the thread taut in your other hand, pull the wraps of thread up the needle and under your thumb and forefinger, holding the eye end. Pull the needle through the loops to make a neat knot. Insert the needle directly below where you want to start to embroider.

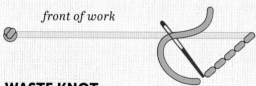

front of work

WASTE KNOT

For this temporary knot, knot the end of your thread on the front of the fabric, and then take the thread to the back of the fabric, about 3 or 4 inches (7–10 cm) away from where you're going to make your first stitch. Bring the thread to the front again to start embroidering. When done, cut the knot off and thread away on the back as you would to finish.

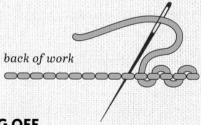

back of work

FINISHING OFF

End off a row by taking your thread to the back of the fabric and securing it under the stitching. You are, in effect, whipping the back of the stitching. Secure it under a few stitches (at least five, more if necessary). You can also knot the thread, keeping it as close to the back of the fabric as possible, or make a small double stitch if you've used backing fabric.

OUTLINE STITCHES

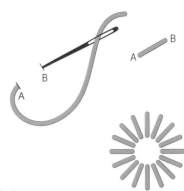

straight stitch

The straight stitch is also known as an isolated satin stitch or stroke stitch. This simple stitch forms the basis of many other stitches, so it's covered first.

1. Come up at A and take your needle down again at B.
2. Pull the thread through until the stitch lies neatly on top of the fabric.

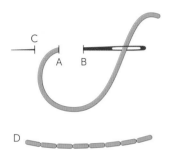

backstitch

The backstitch is good for lines and outlines, especially those with a lot of sharp points.

1. Bring the thread to the front of the fabric at A. Stick your needle into the fabric at B (the start of the line) and out again at C to create the first stitch. Continue in this way to the end of the row, using the same holes in the fabric at the start and end of each stitch.
2. To end the row, take your needle to the back of the fabric at D.

whip stitch

This relatively simple stitch, sometimes called an overcast stitch, involves small diagonal stitches evenly spaced that bind the edge of the fabric.

1. Come up at point A from beneath then loop the thread over the edge of the fabric.
2. Push the needle through the fabric from back to front again, a small distance to the side of the original stitch at B.

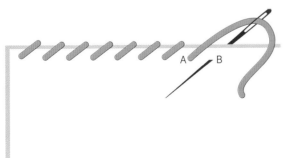

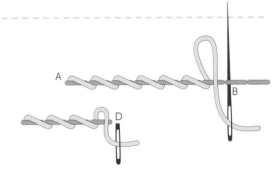

whipped backstitch

This variation of the backstitch is a fun way to add a second color to the line or to add texture.

1. Start by backstitching the line.
2. Take a 2nd thread and needle and come up at the beginning of the line of backstitching at A. Slide the needle under the first backstitch, from right to left, without piercing the fabric. Whip the whole line of stitches in this way.
3. To end off, take your thread to the back to the right of the last backstitch at D.

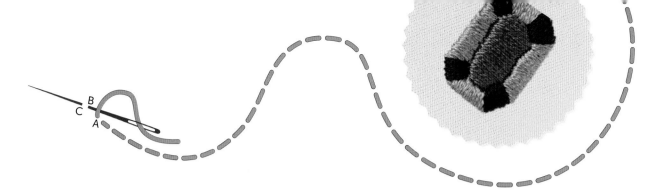

running stitch

Running stitch is a simple stitch that can be spaced in various ways to different effect. Bear in mind when creating your own designs that sections of any line drawn onto your fabric will show, as running stitch doesn't cover the line completely.

1. Bring your thread up at A, then take your needle down at B and reemerge at C.
2. Continue in this way to the end of the row, taking your thread to the back of the fabric to complete the last stitch.
3. Experiment with different lengths of stitches and gaps to create various effects with running stitch.

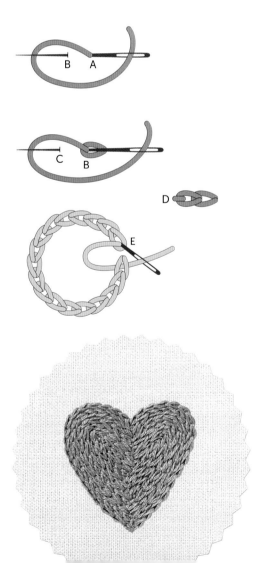

chain stitch

Chain stitch can be used for outlines as well as in rows to fill or partially fill a shape. And it can be whipped in a similar or contrasting color thread to create a new stitch.

1. Bring the thread up at A and then take your needle back down through A and reemerge at B, keeping the thread under the tip of the needle. Pull the thread through until the first chain stitch is neatly looped around the emerging thread. Be careful not to pull too tightly or the stitch will distort. For the second and consecutive chain stitches, take the needle back in at B and reemerge at C.
2. To end off a row, make a small securing stitch by taking the thread down at D. To end off a closed shape such as a circle, come up at E and then slide your needle under the top of the first chain to create a mock chain stitch before taking your thread back down through E.

detached chain stitch

Detached chain stitches are simply isolated chain stitches. They can be stitched along a line or arranged in rows to fill an area of a design. They make excellent flower petals and leaves.

1. Bring the thread up at A and then take your needle back down through A and reemerge at B, keeping the thread under the tip of the needle. Pull the thread through until the chain stitch is neatly looped around the emerging thread. Be careful not to pull too tightly or the stitch will distort.
2. Take the thread back down at C to complete the detached chain stitch.

lazy daisy stitch

Detached chain stitches arranged in a flower shape are known as lazy daisy stitches. You can keep them separate and fill the center with one or more French knots, or come up through the same hole in the center each time.

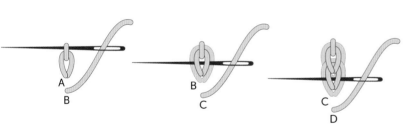

Hungarian chain stitch

This variation of the chain stitch, also called the braided chain stitch, creates an even thicker, raised line.

1. Create a detatched chain stitch to start. Bring the needle back out through point B and then thread it under the anchor stitch of the detached chain stitch and then put the needle back in through point B, creating another loop.
2. Bring the needle up through C. Take the thread over the outside loop and under the inside loop. Put the needle back through C to finish the loop.
3. Bring the needle up through D and continue the pattern.

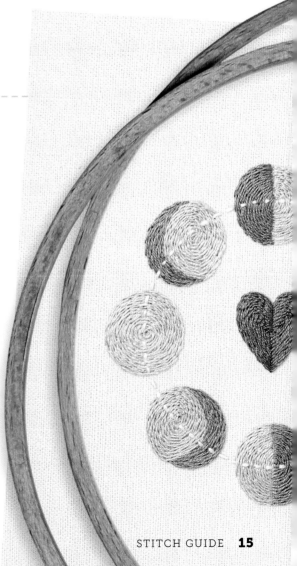

twisted chain stitch

Twisted chain stitch is a beautifully textured stitch and can be used to embroider a single row or to fill a shape. Keep the length of each individual stitch as consistent as possible to create a neat row of embroidery.

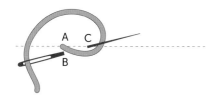

1. Bring your needle and thread up through the fabric at A. Insert your needle at B—a little to the left of A—and bring it up again on the line at C. Loop your thread around the tip of the needle. Pull the thread through to form the first twisted chain stitch.
2. Insert your needle at D, outside the first twisted chain stitch, and bring it up again on the line at E. Loop your thread around the needle tip and pull it through. Continue to the end of the row.
3. Finish with a small securing stitch over the lower edge of the last twisted chain stitch in the row, from F to G.

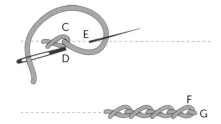

couching

Couching, sometimes called laid work, is where the main thread is placed on the fabric in the desired shape and then tacked down using short stitches.

1. Bring the needle of the main thread up through the back of the fabric at point A and take it back down at the end of the pattern line that is to be worked, point B. Make sure that you this long stitch loose especially if the line that is to be worked is curved.
2. With a new thread (either in the same or a contrasting color) tack the main thread down to the fabric using short straight stitches that cross over the main thread. To make these tacking stitches come up at one side of the main thread, point C, cross the main thread and go down on the other side, point D. Repeat making even tack stitches until the length of main thread is secured to the fabric.

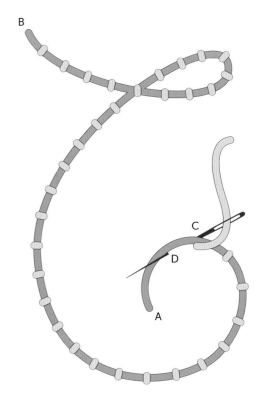

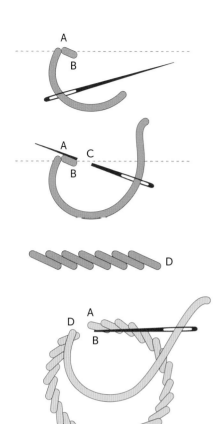

stem stitch

Stem stitch is good for outlines. The tricks are to bring your needle up through the hole at the end of the prior stitch and to always keep your thread below your needle. Use even stitch lengths for a neat row. Done correctly, stem stitch forms a row of backstitch on the back of your work. Bring your thread up at A and, working from left to right, make the first stitch from B to A. Your thread should reemerge through the same hole at A.

1. Keep your thread below your needle at all times and make the next stitch from C to B, bringing your needle up through the same hole at B. Continue stitching along the line in this way.

2. To end off a row of stem stitch, make the last stitch from D to C and then take the needle back down at D. You can omit this last half stitch and take your needle down straight at D when making the last stitch (using this method will leave a thinner section at the end of the row). For a closed shape such as a circle, make the last stitch from A to D and then take your needle back down again at B (covering your first small stitch) to hide the join.

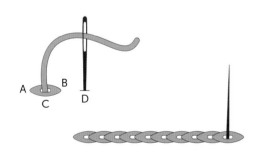

split stitch

1. Make a small stitch (A − B)
2. Bring the needle up through the center of the stitch was just made (C) and come down again with a straight stitch the same length as the first stitch at D. Repeat.

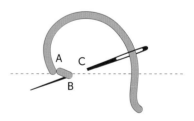

outline stitch

The outline stitch is very similar to the stem stitch, they both create twisted lines that are perfect for outlining objects. The difference between the two is that For outline stitch, the loop of working thread stays on the top, and for stem stitch, the loop of working thread stays on the bottom.

FILL STITCHES

seed stitch

Seed stitches are a "confetti-like" group of small single straight stitches of uniform length that can add decorative texture or, when stitched densely together, can fill a shape.

1. An individual seed stitch is worked as a small straight stitch about 2-3mm long. After completing the first seed stitch, work the next stitch in the same way, in a different direction. Concentrate on making sure the stitches next to each other face a different way in order to create a random effect.

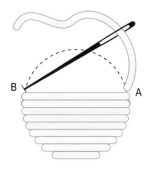
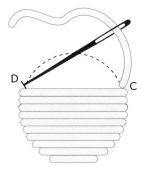

satin stitch

Satin stitch fills an area with straight stitches. To make it easier, do it as a stab stitch: bring your thread up through the fabric and take it down in two actions.

1. Begin in the middle of the area you want to fill and stitch outward, then return to the center and fill the other half. The shape to be filled dictates the direction of your stitches. Follow any curves by increasing the space between stitches along one edge and decreasing on the other.
2. Bring your thread to the front of the fabric at A and take it down again at B as you would to make a straight stitch. Come up again at C and take your thread to the back again at D to create the next stitch.
3. Continue in this way until the entire area is filled with dense stitching.

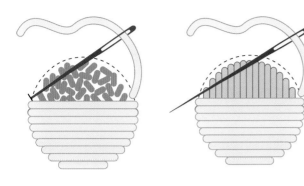

padded satin stitch

Padded satin stitch is made up of layers of satin stitching.

1. Start with a layer that doesn't quite reach the outlines of the final shape. Then embroider another layer of satin stitch over this, filling the shape. You can use two, three, or more layers to give added height. Embroider each layer perpendicular to the last.

long short stitch

This stitch is popular way to fill areas and create color gradients.

1. Start by making a long straight stitch. Stitch number 2 will be a short stitch (approximately half the size of the long stitch). Alternate creating parallel long and short stitches along the edge of the area to be filled.
2. For the next row of stitches, you will make straight stitches that are all the same length, though their placement will vary because of the alternating lengths of the stitches in the previous row. Make as many rows as needed to fill the design.
3. To finish the section, create a row of corresponding long and short stitches so that the stitches create an even finished edge.

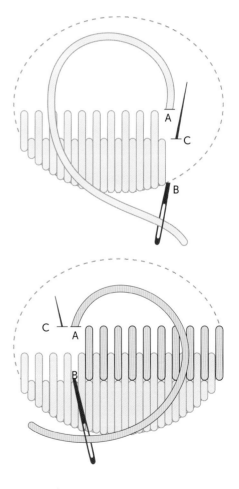

DECORATIVE STITCHES & TECHNIQUES

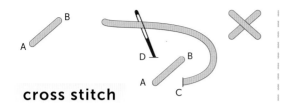

cross stitch

Cross stitch is probably the most familiar embroidery stitch. It can be worked as an isolated stitch or in rows. The four points of each cross-stitch should form a square.

1. Bring your thread up at A and down at B to create the first half of the cross.
2. Bring the needle up at C and take it down again at D to complete the stitch.
3. Pull the thread through until the cross lies neatly on the fabric.

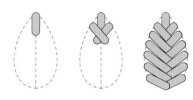

fishbone leaf

The fishbone stitch is very useful for making leaf shapes.
1. Make a straight stitch from the top point of the leaf shape to the bottom.
2. Make stitch number 2 from the top left side of the line, down and across the center line to the right, about ¼ inch long.
3. Make stitch number 3 from the top right side of the line, down and across the center line to the left.
4. Make stitch number 4 directly below stitch number 1, following the pattern lines, and continue the crossing stitches until the leaf is complete.

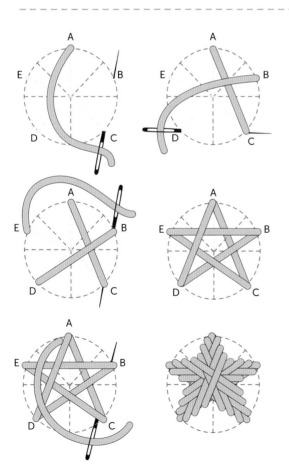

woven star stitch

1. Start by drawing a circle the size you want your finished star. Mark five even dots around the circle.
2. ring thread up through the fabric at point A and down at C then back up at B. From B, bring the stitch down at D. Bring the thread back up at C and down at E. Next stitch up from E and down at B. Continue this pattern of bringing the thread up at one point, skipping the next point around the circle and bringing it down at the next point until the star takes shape.
3. To form the second layer of the woven star, bring the thread up at point A, this time slightly to the left of the original stitch. Follow the same pattern as before, each time placing the stitch slightly to the left of the first round of stitches.
4. Repeat this pattern. Each time you bring the thread up and back down stay on the left side of the point and move down the star points until you reach the center of the star.

star stitch

Star stitch is an isolated stitch that can be scattered randomly over an area or worked in a grid pattern for a more uniform look. It can be caught down in the middle with a small cross-stitch, too, if you prefer.

1. Come up at A. Stick your needle into the fabric at B and reemerge at C. Pull your thread through to make the first stitch.
2. Do the same from D to E and F to G, then take your thread to the back at H.
3. Complete the star stitch by catching it down with a small stitch from I to J.

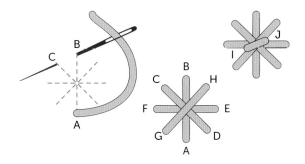

turkey stitch

This stitch, also called turkey work stitch or Ghiordes knot, is used to create three dimensional fringe and is used to great effect on the Leo lion's mane.

1. Start stitching through the top of the fabric at A and leaving ½ to 1" tail of thread sticking out of the top of the fabric.
2. Come up through the fabric create a backstitch (from B to C) to anchor the thread tail. A, being sure to hold that tail and not pull it through. Then come up and anchor that tail with a backstitch (B-C).
3. Come up at D, right next to A under the backstitch. Go down at E, a stitch length away but leave a loop of thread on the top of the fabric. The shorter the stitch length from D to E the more concentrated the tufted knots per inch.
4. Stitch an anchor backstitch over that insertion point to secure (F to G). Repeat.
5. Once you are finished stitching, use scissors to cut the tops of the loops to create a fringe effect. Tease the thread fringe to fluff out the thread if desired.

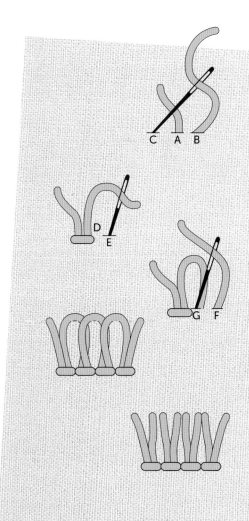

KNOTS

French knot (double)

To create French knots, it helps to use a milliner/straw needle for knots.

1. Bring your thread up at A. Hold your needle in one hand and wrap the thread over the needle twice with the other.
2. Hold the thread taut so the wraps don't slip off the end of the needle and twist it around to stick into your fabric at B—close to A, but not through the same hole. Pull the wraps of thread taut around the needle so that they lie against the fabric and—keeping hold of your thread so the wraps don't come loose—pull your needle through to the back, drawing the thread through the loops to create the knot.

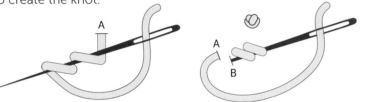

single French knot

In this variation, follow the instructions above but only wrap the thread around the needle once. This creates a more petite thread knot.

triple French knot

This variation on the French knot that creates a larger thread knot. To make a triple French knot, follow the traditional French knot instructions but wrap the thread around the needle three times.

bullion knot

Use a milliner/straw needle to create bullion knots. Although bullion knots can be tricky at first, once you get the hang of them, you'll find these versatile knots can be used as isolated stitches or packed together to fill an area with textured stitching.

1. Bring your thread to the front of the fabric at A. Take your needle to the back at B and reemerge at A. (Take care not to split the thread.)
2. Hold the eye of the needle against the fabric with your left thumb and use your right hand to wrap the thread around the tip of the needle until the length of wound thread measures the same as the distance between A and B. Keep the wraps even but not too tight around the needle. Holding the wraps of the knot between your thumb and forefinger, pull the needle and thread through the wraps. (If you struggle with this step, rotate your needle in the opposite direction of the wraps to loosen them or try a bigger needle.)
3. Keep pulling the thread through the wraps until the top of the knot folds back toward B. If necessary, run your needle under the wraps while pulling on the thread to even them out. Take your thread to the back of the fabric at B to secure the knot.

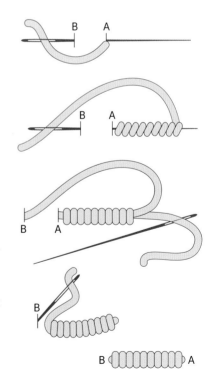

APPLIQUE

Use this technique to fill pattern shapes with custom cut pieces of fabric. Fusible webbing can be found at most chain fabric stores. The most common brands found are Pellon's Wonder Under and Therm-O-Web's HeatnBond.

1. Place a piece of fusible webbing with the rough side up, onto your pattern and trace the shape you wish to applique. Once you have traced the shape, cut around it leaving a ¼" to ½" border.

2. With the wrong side of the fabric facing you, place the shape rough side down on the fabric. Iron the shape using the heat settings indicated on the fusible web's packaging.

3. Once the shape is adhered to the fabric, take scissors and carefully cut the shape out of the fabric.

4. Remove the paper backing from the shape. This will expose the 2nd side of fusible webbing.

5. With both fabrics right-sides up, Iron the applique shape onto the main background fabric where the pattern indicates.

6. Once adhered, stitch the edge of the applique using the stitch indicated in the pattern. Often this is a blanket, satin, or running stitch.

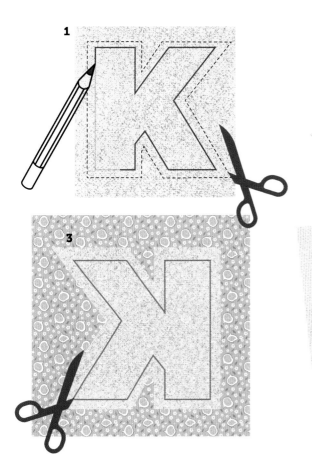

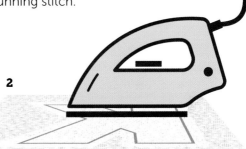

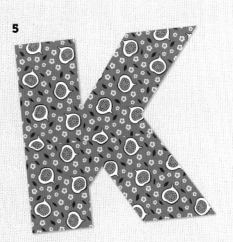

ZODIACS

These colorful patterns use symmetrical imagery to reflect the rich dualities of the twelve signs of the Western zodiac.

ARIES

March 21 - April 19

Aries is the first sign in the Western zodiac and these competitive,
headstrong rams wouldn't have it any other way. Ambitious and driven,
Aries are eager to face any challenge and come out on top.

SYMBOL: THE RAM / ELEMENT: FIRE / RULING PLANET: MARS

DMC FLOSS COLORS:

154 | 166
168 | 310
327 | 469
498 | 608
666 | 740
742 | 777
797 | 936
3760 | 3804
3844 | B5200

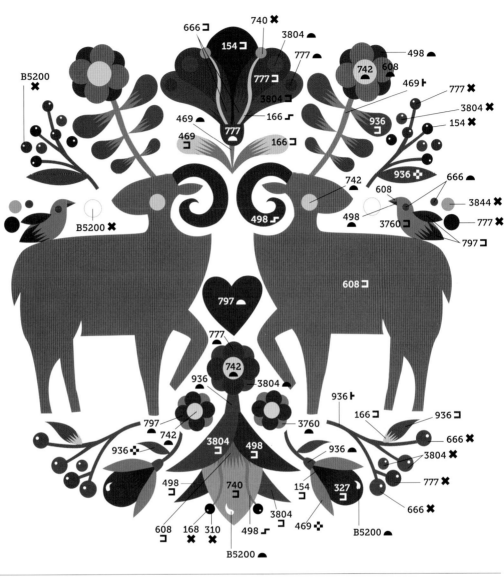

TEMPLATE ON PAGE 100

STITCHING TIPS:

1. Begin by filling the two rams with long short stitches.

2. Use a split backstitch to create the various flower stems.

3. Stitch the French knots and smallest satin stitch areas last.

STITCH KEY:

(see Stitch Guide beginning on page 12 for stitch instructions)

❖ fishbone leaf	✖ French knot(s)	⊐ long short stitch	⏺ satin stitch	⊢ split stitch
⌐ stem stitch				

Pattern stitched by Aly Kostecki

TAURUS

April 20-May 20

Even keeled and occasionally stubborn, Taurus brings stability and serenity to all aspects of their life. They are known to be loyal, patient, and resourceful friends.

SYMBOL: THE BULL / ELEMENT: EARTH / RULING PLANET: VENUS

DMC FLOSS COLORS:

208	310
327	469
498	608
718	740
742	777
797	936
939	959
814	3804
B5200	154

TEMPLATE ON PAGE 101

STITCHING TIPS:

1. The long short stitches used to fill the bulls flow from the head down towards the legs following the curves of the bulls.

2. Use a split backstitch to create the various flower stems.

3. The berries and white dots seen throughout the pattern are created using clusters of small French knots.

STITCH KEY:

(see Stitch Guide beginning on page 12 for stitch instructions)

❖ fishbone leaf	✖ French knot(s)	⅃ long short stitch	◣ satin stitch	⊢ split stitch
⌐ stem stitch				

Pattern stitched by Aly Kostecki

GEMINI

May 21-June 21

The chatty, mercurial Geminis excel in all forms of communication. They have an innate mastery of language, music, and social skills. With insatiable curiosity and energy they seem to get twice as much done as the rest of us.

SYMBOL: THE TWINS / ELEMENT: AIR / RULING PLANET: MERCURY

DMC FLOSS COLORS:

29, 154, 166, 168, 310, 469, 498, 608, 666, 718, 742, 777, 797, 934, 936, 939, 950, 3771, 3804, 3760

TEMPLATE ON PAGE 102

STITCHING TIPS:

1. For each twin, start at their waist and have the long short stitches follow their curves eventually ending at the feet.

2. Use a split backstitch to create the various flower stems.

3. The berries and centers of the round flowers seen throughout the pattern are created using clusters of small French knots.

STITCH KEY:

(see Stitch Guide beginning on page 12 for stitch instructions)

✖ French knot(s)	⅃ long short stitch	⬥ satin stitch	⌐ stem stitch	■ straight stitch

Pattern stitched by Emilie Ganiere

CANCER
Dates: June 22- July 21

Intuitive and emotional, Cancers enjoy time with their (chosen) family. They excel at creating nurturing, cozy environments and are deeply attached to the people close to them.

SYMBOL: THE CRAB / ELEMENT: WATER / RULING PLANET: MOON

DMC FLOSS COLORS:

29
154   166
151   208
310   321
469   498
608   666
740   777
797   934
936   939
3804 3760

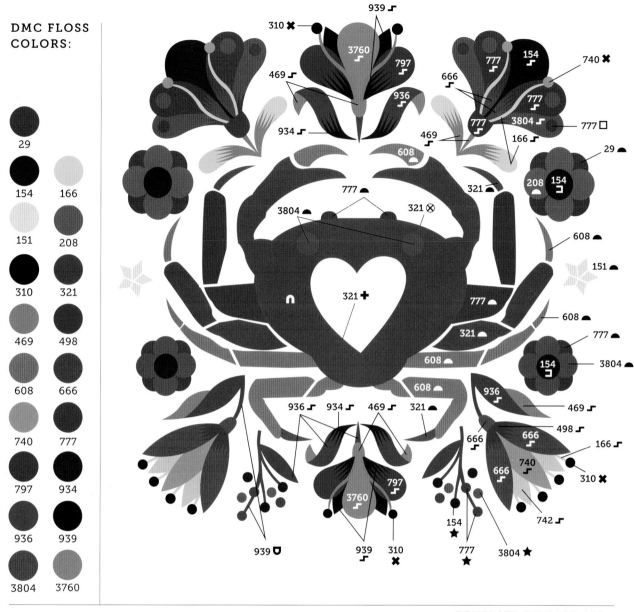

TEMPLATE ON PAGE 103

STITCHING TIPS:

1. Trace and cut out the body of the crab in red fabric.

2. Stitch the red crab body applique to the main fabric using decorative cross stitches and use whip stitches to attach the heart cutout to the main fabric.

STITCH KEY:

(See Stitch Guide beginning on page 12 for stitch instructions)

∩ applique	● backstitch	⊔ couching	⊗ cross stitch	✖ French knot(s)
⅂ long short stitch	☐ padded satin stitch	◖ satin stitch	★ star stitch	⌐ stem stitch
✛ whip stitch				

Pattern stitched by Megan Potter

LEO

July 22-August 22

The regal Leo loves being the center of attention and admiration. They can be passionate, theatrical, and a touch vain, as there is no spotlight too big or small for them to bask in.

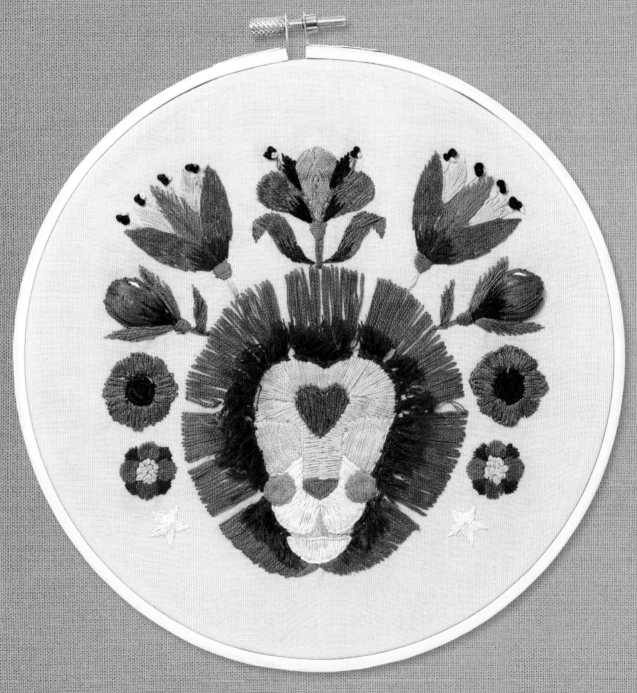

SYMBOL: LION / ELEMENT: FIRE / RULING PLANET: SUN

DMC FLOSS COLORS:

154 166
168 310
327 335
350 422
437 469
498 608
666 677
742 777
797 934
936 939
3760 3804
B5200

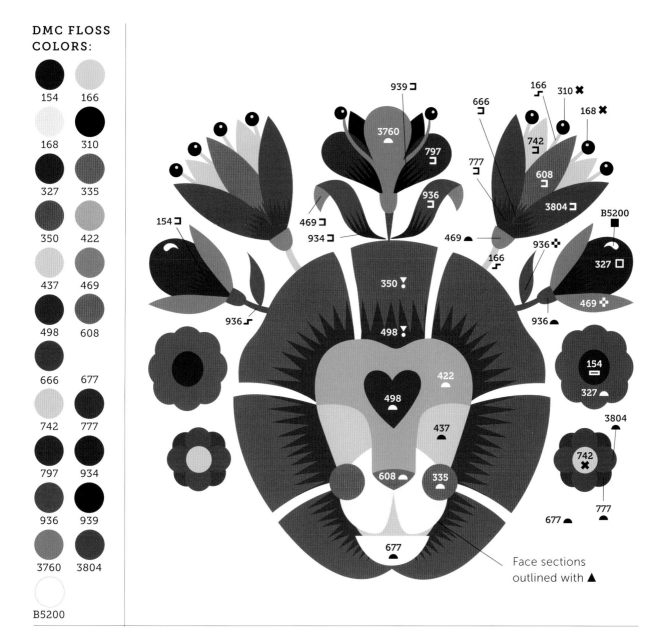

Face sections outlined with ▲

TEMPLATE ON PAGE 104

STITCHING TIPS:

1. Have the satin stitching on the lion's forehead radiate out from around the heart to the edge of the main.

2. Use turkey stitches to create the lion's fringed mane.

3. The center of the purple flowers are made using bullion knots that increase in size as they go from the center outward towards the petals.

STITCH KEY:

(see Stitch Guide beginning on page 12 for stitch instructions)

▬ bullion knot(s)	✛ fishbone leaf	✖ French knot(s)	⊐ long short stitch	☐ padded satin stitch
▲ satin stitch	⌐ stem stitch	■ straight stitch	❗ turkey stitch	▲ whipped backstitch

Pattern stitched by Erica Ingram

VIRGO

August 23 – September 22

Virgos are known as logical, sensible and take a practical approach to life. They are happy to put in the time and practice if it means they can get the perfect outcome.

SYMBOL: THE MAIDEN / ELEMENT EARTH / RULING PLANET MERCURY

DMC FLOSS COLORS:

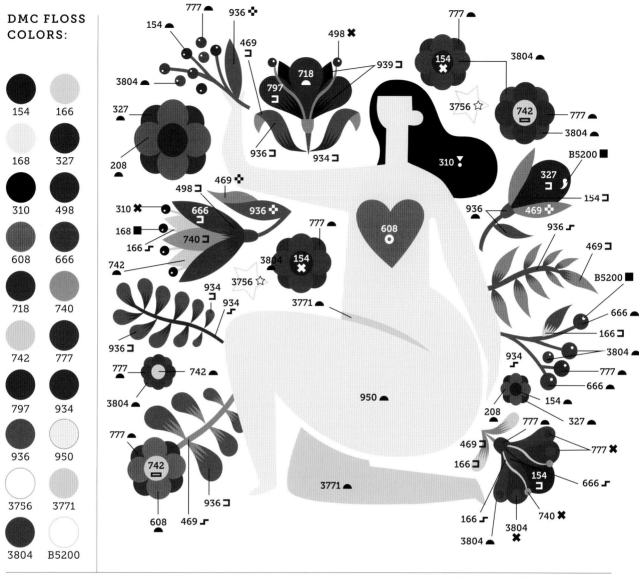

154 | 166
168 | 327
310 | 498
608 | 666
718 | 740
742 | 777
797 | 934
936 | 950
3756 | 3771
3804 | B5200

TEMPLATE ON PAGE 105

STITCHING TIPS:

1. The large purple flower is created using a stuffed satin stitch. If you would like to create and an even more three-dimensional flower, you can stuff the satin stitch flower with scrap bits of thread or even fiberfill stuffing.

2. After statin stitching Virgo's hair, add turkey stitches to simulate, loose three-dimensional hair.

STITCH KEY:

(see Stitch Guide beginning on page 12 for stitch instructions)

▬ bullion knot(s)	⬤ chain stitch	✤ fishbone leaf	✖ French knot(s)	⌐ long short stitch
◨ outline stitch	☐ padded satin stitch	⬤ satin stitch	⌐ stem stitch	■ straight stitch
❗ turkey stitch	☆ woven star stitch			

Pattern stitched by Erica Ingram

LIBRA

September 23- October 22

The Libra's scales reflect their desire to bring balance to all aspects of their life. They love symmetry and the peace that equilibrium brings them.

SYMBOL: SCALES / ELEMENT: AIR / RULING PLANET: VENUS

DMC FLOSS COLORS:

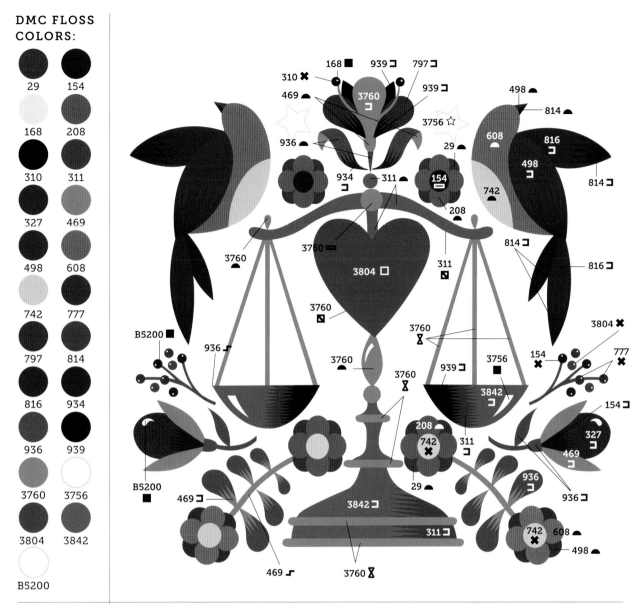

29 · 154 · 168 · 208 · 310 · 311 · 327 · 469 · 498 · 608 · 742 · 777 · 797 · 814 · 816 · 934 · 936 · 939 · 3760 · 3756 · 3804 · 3842 · B5200

TEMPLATE ON PAGE 106

STITCHING TIPS:

1. The heart in the center of the design is created using a padded satin stitch. If you would like to create and an even more three-dimensional heart, you can stuff the heart with scrap bits of thread or even fiberfill stuffing.

2. Add the chain stitched lines of the base of the pedestaled after satin stitching the rest of the base.

STITCH KEY: (see Stitch Guide beginning on page 12 for stitch instructions)

▬ bullion knot(s)	✗ Hungarian chain stitch	✖ French knot(s)	⭘ chain stitch	⅃ long short stitch
◪ outline stitch	☐ padded satin stitch	◖ satin stitch	⌐ stem stitch	■ straight stitch
☆ woven star stitch				

Pattern stitched by Erica Ingram

SCORPIO

October 23 – November 22

Scorpios are perhaps the most often misunderstood sign in the zodiac. They are ambitious, passionate, and often gain power easily but may come across as secretive and controlling.

SYMBOL: SCORPION / ELEMENT WATER / RULING PLANET MARS

DMC FLOSS COLORS:

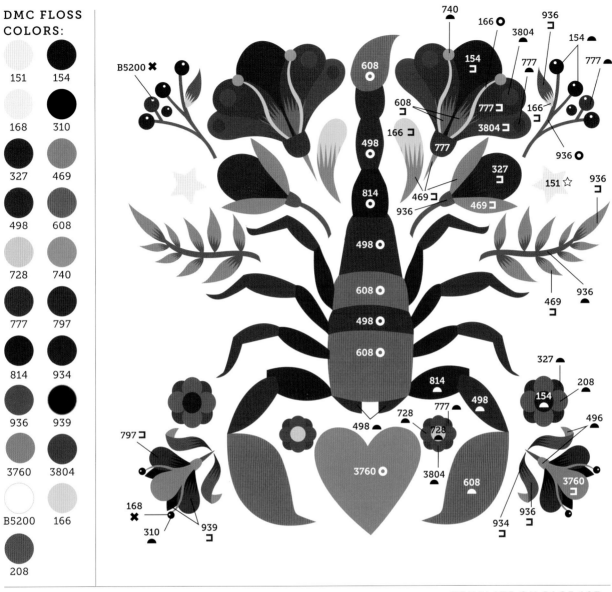

151 | 154
168 | 310
327 | 469
498 | 608
728 | 740
777 | 797
814 | 934
936 | 939
3760 | 3804
B5200 | 166
208

TEMPLATE ON PAGE 107

STITCHING TIPS:

1. The main sections of the scorpion's body are filled using chain stitch. When filling using chain stitch, start on the outside of the shape and continue stitching around the shape working your way towards the center.

2. The light pink stars are created using the woven star stitch.

3. On the larger flowers, add the green chain stitched stamens after you have stitched the main sections of the petals.

STITCH KEY:

(see Stitch Guide beginning on page 12 for stitch instructions)

| ⊙ chain stitch | ✖ French knot(s) | ⊐ long short stitch | ▲ satin stitch | ☆ woven star stitch |

Pattern stitched by Gemma Winter

SAGITTARIUS

November 23 – December 21

The adventuresome archer, Sagittarius, is always on the quest for new knowledge, insight and experiences. Their optimism and sense of humor makes them ideal road trip partners!

SYMBOL: ARCHER / ELEMENT FIRE / RULING PLANET JUPITER

DMC FLOSS COLORS:

29 151
154 166
168 208
310 327
469 608
666 742
777 797
934 936
939 3760
3799 3804
B5200

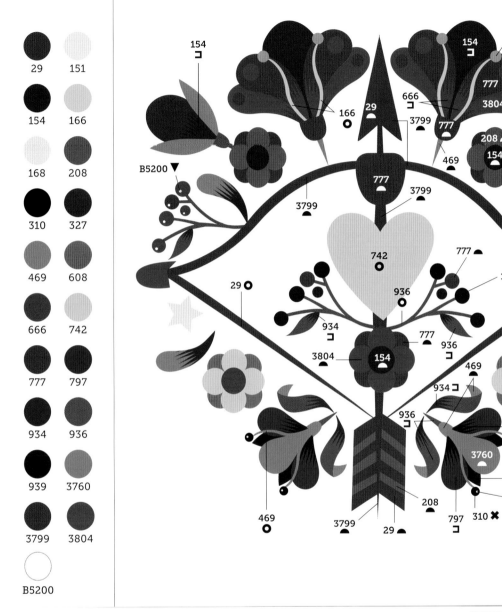

TEMPLATE ON PAGE 108

STITCHING TIPS:

1. Add the chain stitched flower details after you have completed the petals.

2. Stitch the French knots and smallest satin stitch areas last.

STITCH KEY:

(see Stitch Guide beginning on page 12 for stitch instructions)

O chain stitch	✖ French knot(s)	⊐ long short stitch	◖ satin stitch	☆ woven star stitch

Pattern stitched by Gemma Winter

CAPRICORN

December 22 – January 20

Capricorns will take command and get the job done!
These reliable and authoritative goats
can may sometimes come across as know-it-alls.

SYMBOL: GOAT / ELEMENT EARTH / RULING PLANET SATURN

DMC FLOSS COLORS:

- 29
- 154
- 166
- 208
- 310
- 312
- 469
- 498
- 666
- 740
- 742
- 777
- 823
- 936
- 3804
- B5200

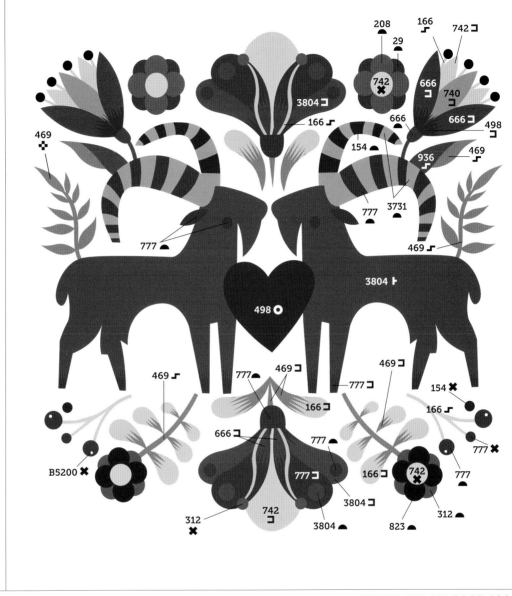

TEMPLATE ON PAGE 109

STITCHING TIPS:

1. Use long short stitches to create the woolly goats.
2. Stitch the French knots and smallest satin stitch areas last.

STITCH KEY: (see Stitch Guide beginning on page 12 for stitch instructions)

⦿ chain stitch	✚ fishbone leaf	✖ French knot(s)	⌐ long short stitch	▲ satin stitch
⊢ split stitch	⌐ stem stitch			

Pattern stitched by Dominique Miyake

AQUARIUS

January 20 — February 18

Aquarius is a breath of fresh air! They effortlessly innovate and are brilliant visionaries but at their worst they can seem distant, cold, and anti-social.

SYMBOL: WATER BEARER / ELEMENT: AIR / RULING PLANET: SATURN

DMC FLOSS COLORS:

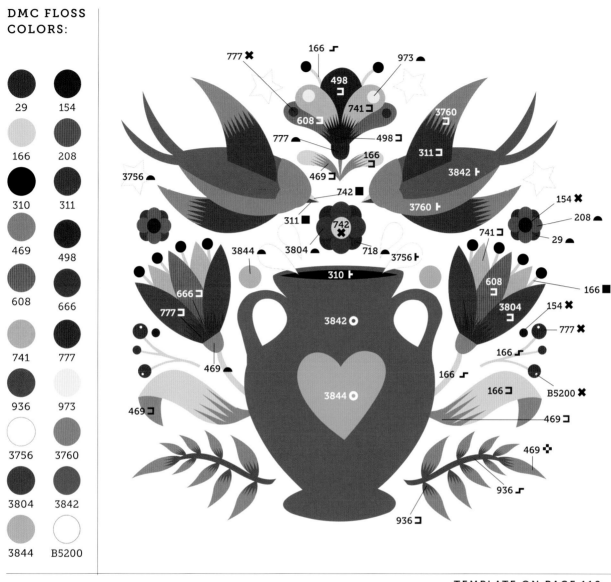

29 154
166 208
310 311
469 498
608 666
741 777
936 973
3756 3760
3804 3842
3844 B5200

TEMPLATE ON PAGE 110

STITCHING TIPS:

1. The shape of the pitcher is filled in using a thick, 3-strand, chain stitch. This stitch adds extra texture and movement to the piece. Begin by stitching the outline of the pitcher shape. Continue to stitch moving clockwise and towards the center of the pitcher until the area is filled.

2. The star shapes are divided into 5 diamond points and can be filled using a diagonal satin stitch.

3. Stitch the French knots and smallest satin stitch areas last.

STITCH KEY: (see Stitch Guide beginning on page 12 for stitch instructions)

O chain stitch	**✤** fishbone leaf	**✖** French knot(s)	**⊐** long short stitch	**⌒** satin stitch
� split stitch	**⌐** stem stitch	**■** straight stitch	**☆** woven star stitch	

Pattern stitched by Dominique Miyake

PISCES

February 19- March 20

Ever the optimist, Pisces is swimming in a glass half full. These gentle fish are artistic and compassionate to the point of being self-sacrificing.

SYMBOL: FISH / ELEMENT WATER / RULING PLANET: JUPITER

DMC FLOSS COLORS:

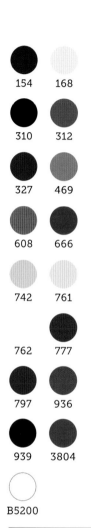

154 168
310 312
327 469
608 666
742 761
762 777
797 936
939 3804
B5200

TEMPLATE ON PAGE 111

STITCHING TIPS:

1. Twisted chain stitches add a nice texture to the striped sections of the fish. Make sure they run horizontally along the length of the fish to contrast with the satin stitches.

2. To get a neat uniform look in the larger satin stitch areas, make sure your threads do not twist.

STITCH KEY:

(see Stitch Guide beginning on page 12 for stitch instructions)

✤ fishbone leaf	✖ French knot(s)	⊐ long short stitch	◖ satin stitch	⊦ split stitch
◆ twisted chain stitch				

Pattern stitched by Abbi Sawyer

ZODIAC PATTERNS **49**

CELESTIAL PATTERNS

The following patterns are inspired by the beauty, mystery, and insight that can be found at night.

MIDNIGHT
BAT

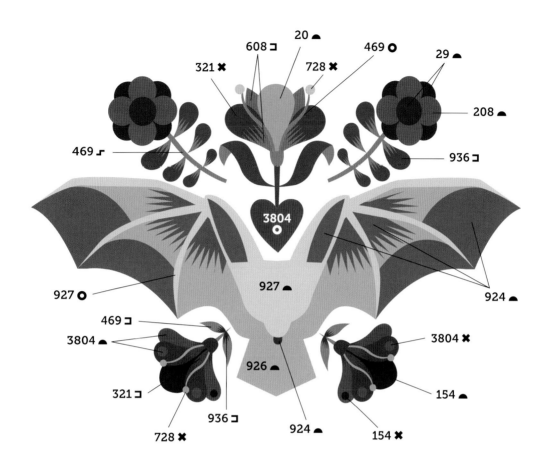

DMC FLOSS COLORS:

20   29   154   208   321   469   608   728   924   926   927   936   3804

TEMPLATE ON PAGE 111

STITCHING TIPS:

1. When stitching the wings, make sure the direction of the stitches on the left wing is mirrored on the right wing.

2. Chain stitch the wing ridges after satin stitching the main sections of the wings.

STITCH KEY: (see Stitch Guide beginning on page 12 for stitch instructions)

O chain stitch	**✖** French knot(s)	**⊐** long short stitch	**▲** satin stitch	**⌐** stem stitch

Pattern stitched by Dominique Miyake

LUNA MOTH

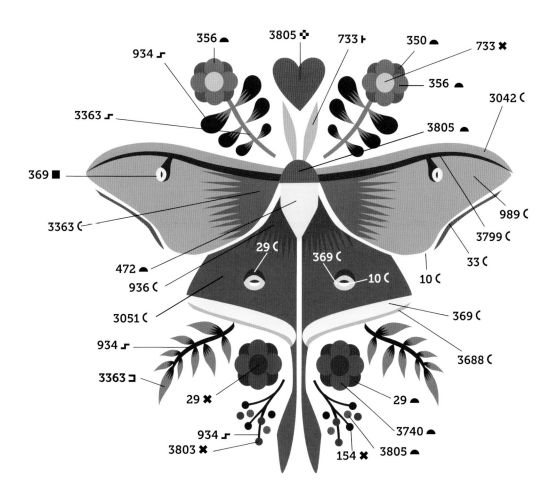

DMC FLOSS COLORS:

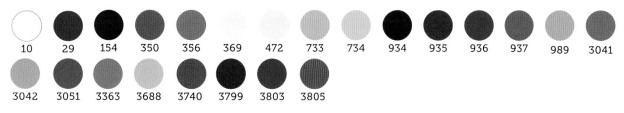

| 10 | 29 | 154 | 350 | 356 | 369 | 472 | 733 | 734 | 934 | 935 | 936 | 937 | 989 | 3041 |

| 3042 | 3051 | 3363 | 3688 | 3740 | 3799 | 3803 | 3805 |

TEMPLATE ON PAGE 111

STITCHING TIPS:

1. To stitch the heard using the fishbone leaf stitch, imagine that the point of the heard is the same as the tip of the leaf.

2. Stitch the French knots at the center of the flowers last.

STITCH KEY: (see Stitch Guide beginning on page 12 for stitch instructions)

✿ fishbone leaf	✖ French knot(s)	⌐ long short stitch	◢ satin stitch	(seed stitch
├ split stitch	⌐ stem stitch			

Pattern stitched by Megan Potter

MOONLIGHT
OWL

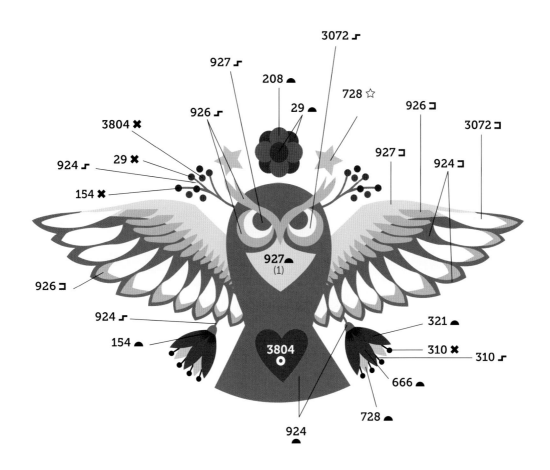

DMC FLOSS COLORS:

29 154 208 310 321 666 728 924 926 927 3072 3804

TEMPLATE ON PAGE 112

STITCHING TIPS:

1. Chain stitch the heart on the owl before you begin satin stitching the body.

2. When stitching the wings, make sure the direction of the stitches on the left wing is mirrored on the right wing.

STITCH KEY: (see Stitch Guide beginning on page 12 for stitch instructions)

O chain stitch	**✖** French knot(s)	**⊐** long short stitch	**▲** satin stitch	**⌐** stem stitch
☆ woven star stitch				

Pattern stitched by Dominique Miyake

PHASES
OF THE MOON

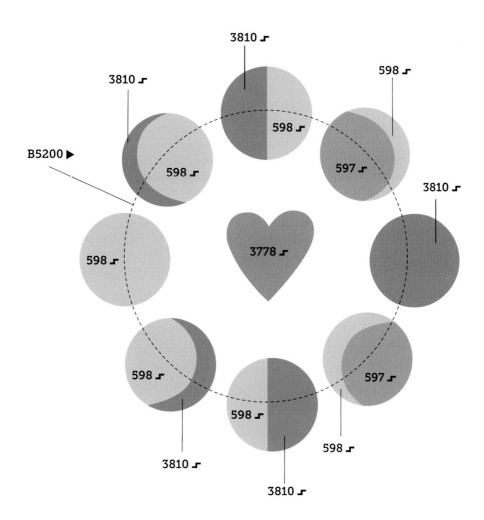

DMC FLOSS COLORS:

597 598 3778 3810 B5200

TEMPLATE ON PAGE 112

STITCHING TIPS:

1. When filling the heart and moon shapes, start in the center of the design and work your way outwards.

2. Stitch the running stitch line after you have completed stem stitching the rest of the design.

STITCH KEY: (see Stitch Guide beginning on page 12 for stitch instructions)

▶ running stitch   ⌐ stem stitch

Pattern stitched by Aly Kostecki

CRYSTALS

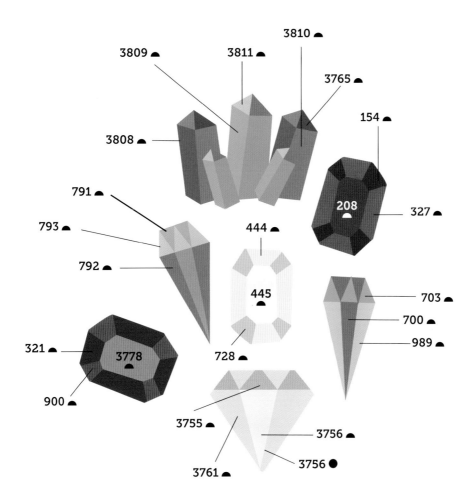

DMC FLOSS COLORS:

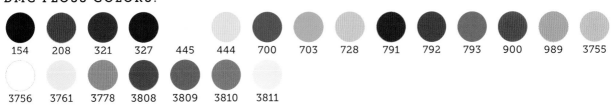

154   208   321   327   445   444   700   703   728   791   792   793   900   989   3755

3756   3761   3778   3808   3809   3810   3811

TEMPLATE ON PAGE 113

STITCHING TIPS:

1. You can pick and choose to stitch a couple of the crystals or the whole group.

2. Backstitch the two lines of the diamond shape after finishing all the satin stitching of the rest of the pattern.

STITCH KEY:

(see Stitch Guide beginning on page 12 for stitch instructions)

● backstitch	▲ satin stitch

Pattern stitched by Gemma Winter

THE PLANETS

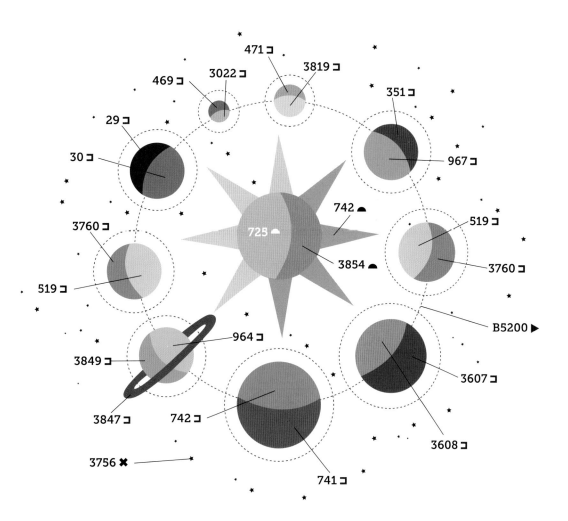

DMC FLOSS COLORS:

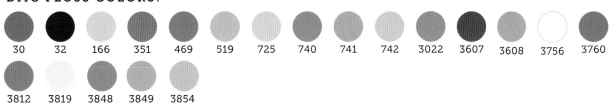

30 32 166 351 469 519 725 740 741 742 3022 3607 3608 3756 3760

3812 3819 3848 3849 3854

TEMPLATE ON PAGE 113

STITCHING TIPS:

1. Backstitch around the planets after you have completed filling them in.

2. The small stars are made using 3756 French knots.

STITCH KEY:
(see Stitch Guide beginning on page 12 for stitch instructions)

● backstitch	✖ French knot(s)	⌐ long short stitch	⏣ satin stitch

Pattern stitched by Erica Ingram

TELESCOPE

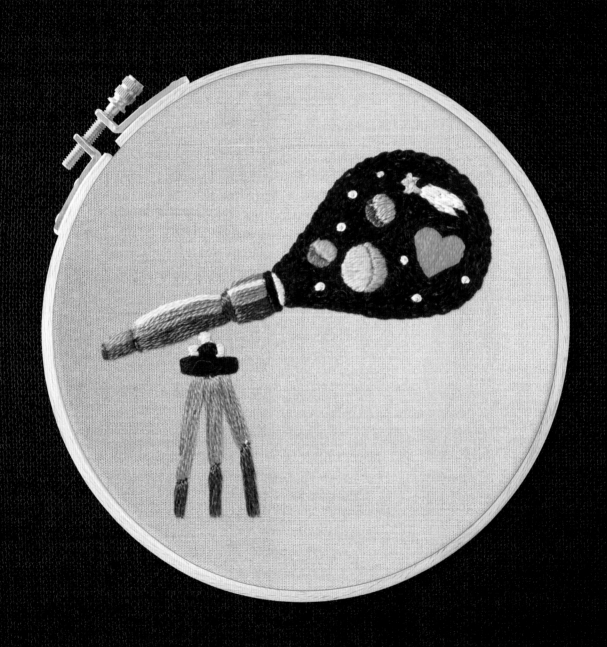

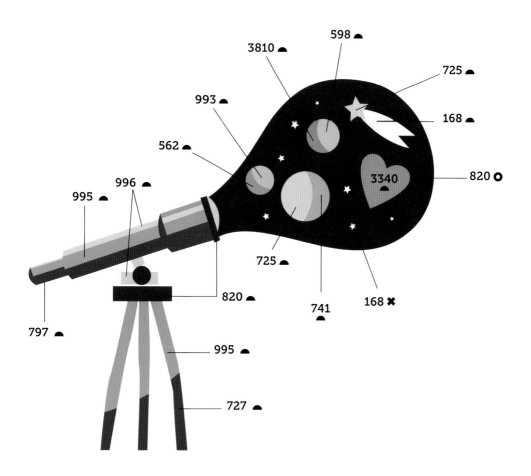

DMC FLOSS COLORS:

| 168 | 562 | 598 | 725 | 741 | 820 | 797 | 995 | 996 | 993 | 3340 | 3810 |

TEMPLATE ON PAGE 114

STITCHING TIPS:

1. Stitch the four small planets and shooting star first, then fill in the black area.

2. Add the small French knot stars last.

STITCH KEY:

(see Stitching Guide beginning on page 12 for stitch instructions)

| **O** chain stitch | **✖** French knot(s) | **⌐** long short stitch | **▲** satin stitch |

Pattern stitched by Gemma Winter

KNOWING
HANDS

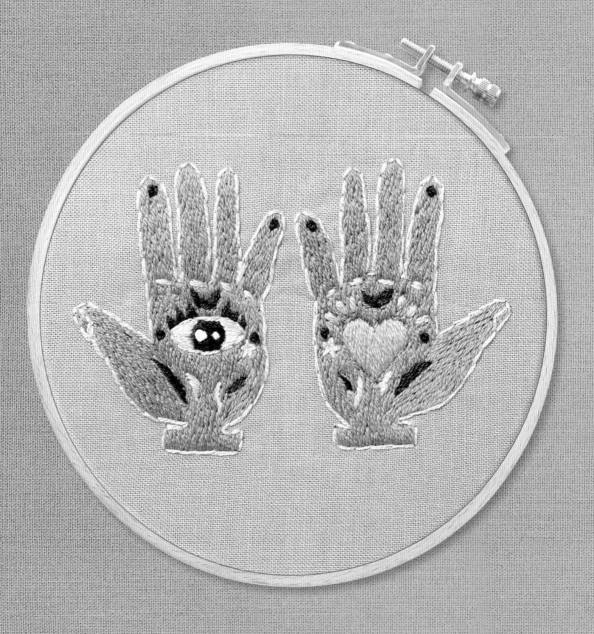

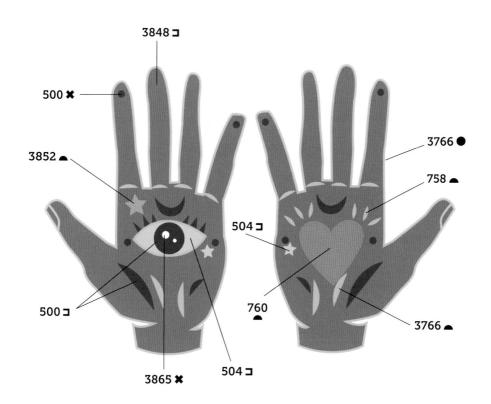

3848 ⌐

500 ✖

3852 ◢

500 ⌐

3865 ✖

504 ⌐

504 ⌐

760 ◢

3766 ●

758 ◢

3766 ◢

DMC FLOSS COLORS:

| 500 | 504 | 758 | 760 | 3766 | 3848 | 3852 | 3865 |

TEMPLATE ON PAGE 114

STITCHING TIPS:

1. Backstitch the outline and accent lines of the hands after you have finished filling in the main sections of the hands with long short stitches.

2. The smallest details, like the highlights of the eye and the eyelashes, should be added last on top of the main stitching.

STITCH KEY: (see Stitch Guide beginning on page 12 for stitch instructions)

| ● backstitch | ✖ French knot(s) | ⌐ long short stitch | ◢ satin stitch |

Pattern stitched by Emilie Ganiere

TINY
TOADSTOOLS

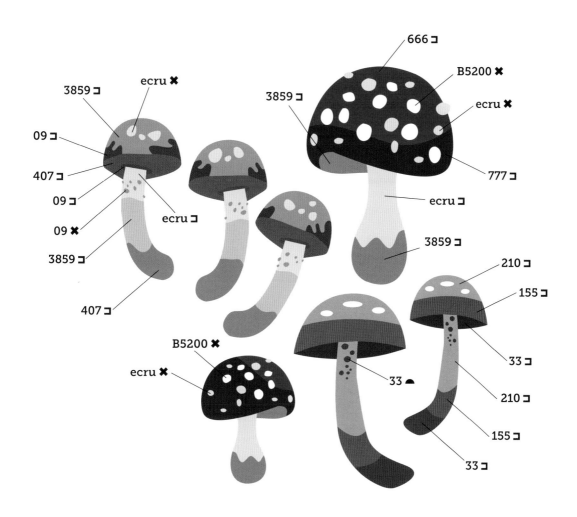

DMC FLOSS COLORS:

| 09 | 33 | 155 | 210 | 407 | 648 | 666 | 777 | 3859 | B5200 | ecru |

TEMPLATE ON PAGE 115

STITCHING TIPS:

1. Add the French knot and small satin stitch dots last after you have completed filling the rest of the area.

2. Make the stitches of the underside of the toadstools radiate out from the stem.

STITCH KEY: (see Stitch Guide beginning on page 12 for stitch instructions)

| ✖ French knot(s) | ❑ long short stitch | ◭ satin stitch |

Pattern stitched by Erica Ingram

SUN

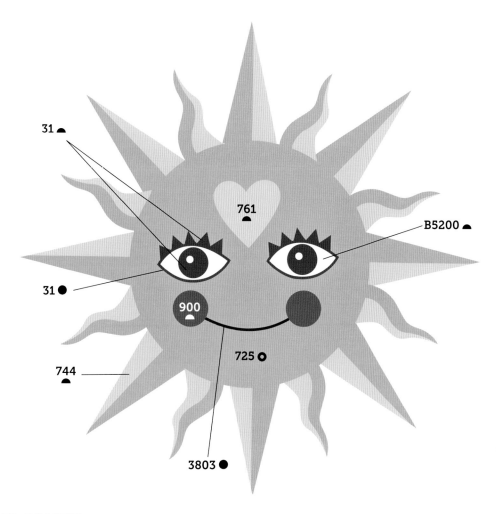

DMC FLOSS COLORS:

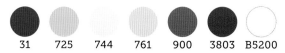

31   725   744   761   900   3803   B5200

TEMPLATE ON PAGE 115

STITCHING TIPS:

1. Chain stitch in a circle starting at the outside of the sun and working your way towards the facial features.

2. Add the details like the eyelashes last.

STITCH KEY: (see Stitch Guide beginning on page 12 for stitch instructions)

● backstitch	O chain stitch	▲ satin stitch

Pattern stitched by Gemma Winter   CELESTIAL PATTERNS   **71**

COMPASS

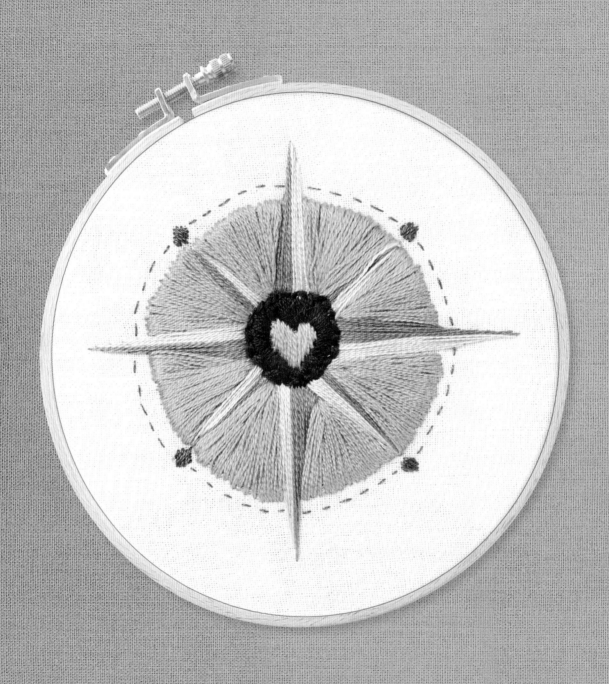

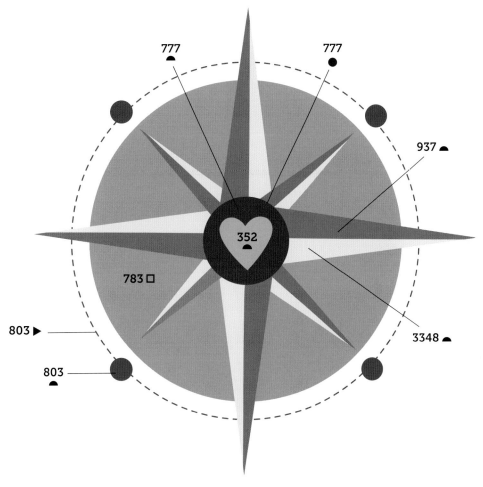

DMC FLOSS COLORS:

352   777   783   803   937   3348

TEMPLATE ON PAGE 116

STITCHING TIPS:

1. For the gold sections, chain stitch the outside portion of the circle before satin stitching over it to create a slight padded satin stitch effect.

2. The blue dots in the orbit line can also be made from large French knots if more three-dimensional elements are desired.

STITCH KEY: (see Stitching Guide beginning on page 12 for stitch instructions)

● backstitch	□ padded satin stitch	▶ running stitch	◢ satin stitch

Pattern stitched by Gemma Winter

BLACK CAT

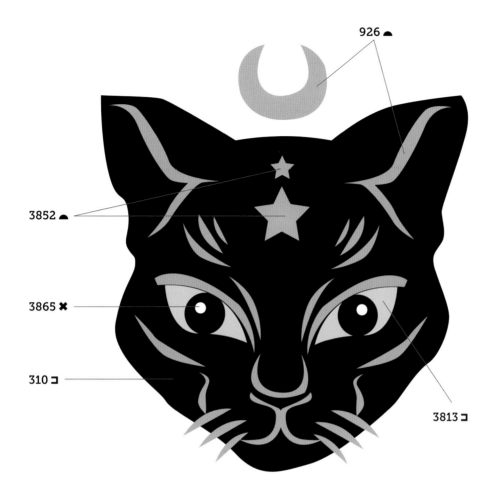

926 ◖

3852 ◖

3865 ✖

310 ⅃

3813 ⅃

DMC FLOSS COLORS:

310   926   3813   3852   3865

TEMPLATE ON PAGE 116

STITCHING TIPS:

1. The smaller star on the cat's forehead can either be created with a satin stitch or a small star stitch.

2. Satin stitch the detail lines after you have completed the main sections of the cat.

STITCH KEY: (see Stitch Guide beginning on page 12 for stitch instructions)

✖ French knot(s)	⅃ long short stitch	◖ satin stitch

Pattern stitched by Emilie Ganiere

LA LUNA

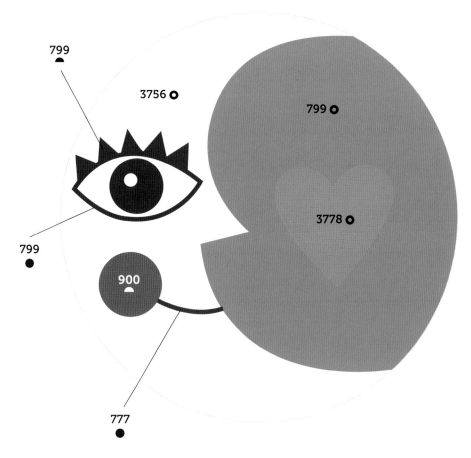

DMC FLOSS COLORS:

777   797   799   900   3778   3756

TEMPLATE ON PAGE 117

STITCHING TIPS:

1. For both the dark blue and light blue sections, Starting at the outside of the pattern, chain stitch around the shape following the curves and working your way inward towards the center.

2. Backstitch the moon's smile last.

STITCH KEY:

(see Stitch Guide beginning on page 12 for stitch instructions)

● backstitch	O chain stitch	▲ satin stitch

Pattern stitched by Gemma Winter

SUMMER FIREFLIES

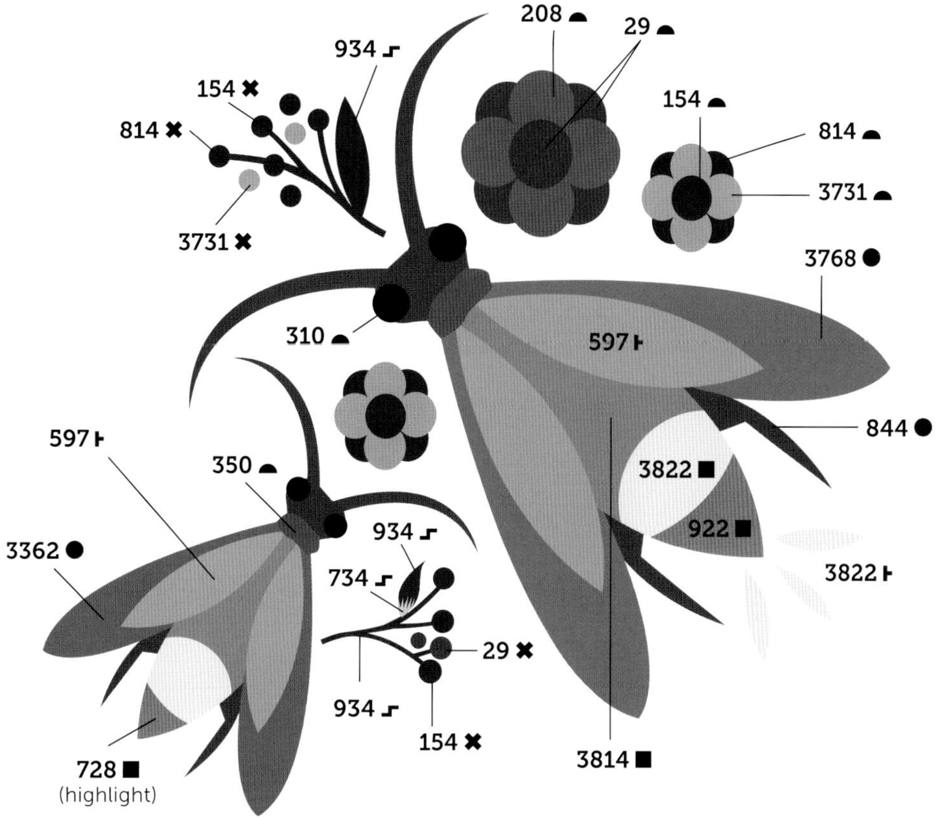
208 ◓
29 ◓
934 ┏
154 ✖
814 ✖
154 ◓
814 ◓
3731 ◓
3731 ✖
3768 ●
310 ◓
597 ⊦
597 ⊦
844 ●
350 ◓
3822 ■
922 ■
3362 ●
934 ┏
3822 ⊦
734 ┏
29 ✖
934 ┏
154 ✖
3814 ■
728 ■
(highlight)

DMC FLOSS COLORS:

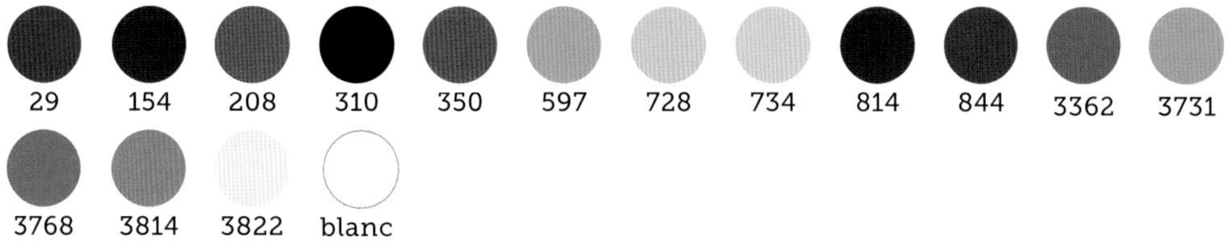
29
154
208
310
350
597
728
734
814
844
3362
3731
3768
3814
3822
blanc

TEMPLATE ON PAGE 117

STITCHING TIPS:

1. The main bodies of the fireflies are created using straight stitch cross-hatching: create a series of 3 or 4 short parallel straight stitches then start another cluster of straight stitches at an adjacent angle of first set of stitches. Continue making adjacent groups of strait stitches until the area is filled.
2. Stitch the fireflies' eyes after the rest of the head.

STITCH KEY:

(see Stitch Guide beginning on page 12 for stitch instructions)

● backstitch	✖ French knot(s)	◓ satin stitch	⊦ split stitch	┏ stem stitch
■ straight stitch				

Pattern stitched by Megan Potter

ZODIAC CONSTELLATIONS

Astrology meets astronomy in these patterns
inspired by the zodiac constellations.

DESIGN YOUR OWN

One of the best parts of embroidery is that it's infinitely customizable! In this section, there are constellations, names, and symbols for each of the twelve zodiac signs. You can stitch them as is or mix-and-match them with some of the previous celestial patterns.

TEMPLATE ON PAGE 119

DMC FLOSS COLORS:

676

729

B5200

STITCH KEY:

♉	couching
⊗	cross stitch
✖	French knot(s)
▶	running stitch
◗	satin stitch
⌐	stem stitch
■	straight stitch

(see Stitch Guide beginning on page 12 for stitch instructions)

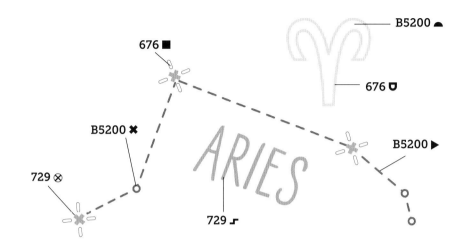

B5200 ◗

676 ■

676 ♉

B5200 ✖

B5200 ▶

729 ⊗

ARIES

729 ⌐

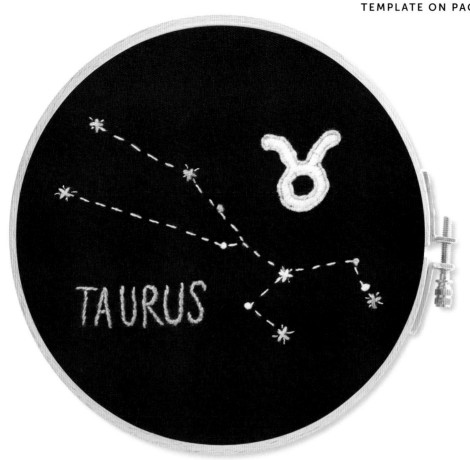

DMC FLOSS COLORS:

676

729   B5200

STITCH KEY:

▽	couching
⊗	cross stitch
✖	French knot(s)
▶	running stitch
◖	satin stitch
⌐	stem stitch
■	straight stitch

(see Stitch Guide
beginning on page 12
for stitch instructions)

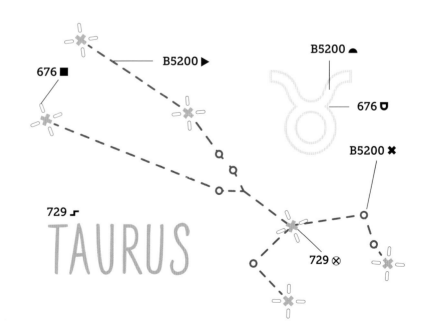

676 ■   B5200 ▶   B5200 ◖

676 ▽

B5200 ✖

729 ⌐   TAURUS   729 ⊗

TEMPLATE ON PAGE 120

DMC FLOSS COLORS:

B5200

STITCH KEY:

●	backstitch
✖	French knot(s)
★	star stitch
⌐	stem stitch

(see Stitch Guide beginning on page 12 for stitch instructions)

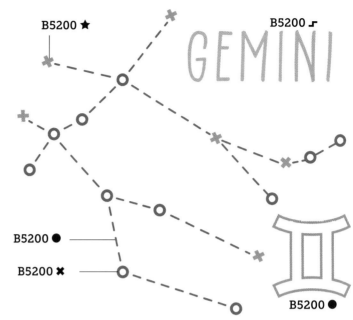

B5200 ★

B5200 ⌐

GEMINI

B5200 ●

B5200 ✖

B5200 ●

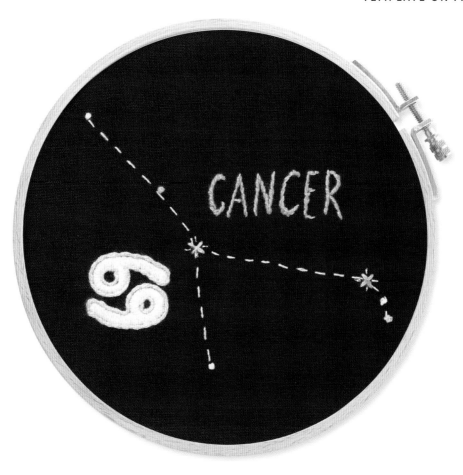

DMC FLOSS COLORS:

676

729

B5200

STITCH KEY:

⛉	couching
⊗	cross stitch
✖	French knot(s)
▶	running stitch
▲	satin stitch
⌐	stem stitch
■	straight stitch

(see Stitch Guide beginning on page 12 for stitch instructions)

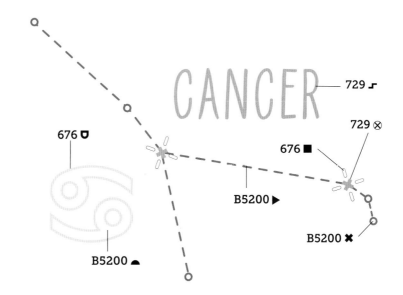

729 ⌐

676 ⛉

729 ⊗

676 ■

B5200 ▶

B5200 ✖

B5200 ▲

DMC FLOSS COLORS:

B5200

STITCH KEY:

●	backstitch
✖	French knot(s)
★	star stitch
⌐	stem stitch
◆	twisted chain stitch

(see Stitch Guide beginning on page 12 for stitch instructions)

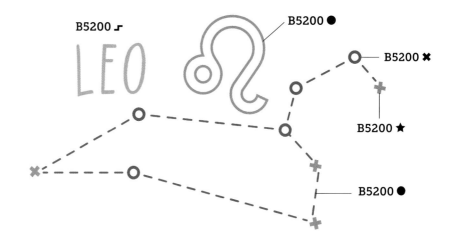

B5200 ⌐

B5200 ●

B5200 ✖

B5200 ★

B5200 ●

DMC FLOSS COLORS:

742   B5200

STITCH KEY:

O	chain stitch
⊗	cross stitch
▶	running stitch
✖	French knot(s)

(see Stitch Guide
beginning on page 12
for stitch instructions)

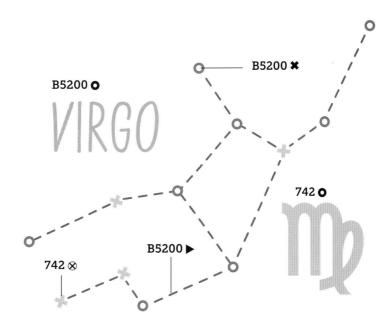

B5200 ✖

B5200 O

VIRGO

742 O

742 ⊗

B5200 ▶

DMC FLOSS COLORS:

742   B5200

STITCH KEY:

O	chain stitch
⊗	cross stitch
✖	French knot(s)
▶	running stitch

(see Stitch Guide beginning on page 12 for stitch instructions)

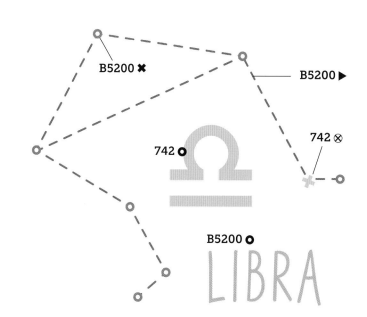

B5200 ✖

B5200 ▶

742 ⊗

742 **O**

B5200 **O**

DMC FLOSS COLORS:

B5200

STITCH KEY:

●	backstitch
✖	French knot(s)
★	star stitch
┎	stem stitch

(see Stitch Guide beginning on page 12 for stitch instructions)

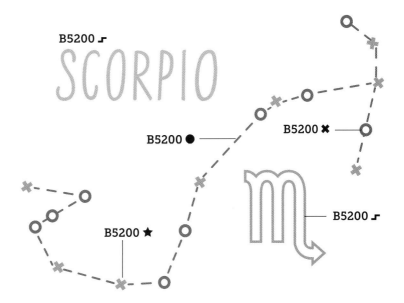

B5200 ┎

SCORPIO

B5200 ●

B5200 ✖

B5200 ┎

B5200 ★

DMC FLOSS COLORS:

742   B5200

STITCH KEY:

⊙	chain stitch
⊗	cross stitch
✖	French knot(s)
▶	running stitch

(see Stitch Guide beginning on page 12 for stitch instructions)

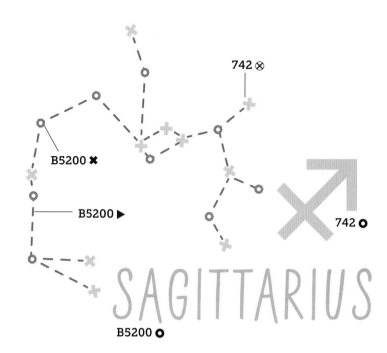

742 ⊗

B5200 ✖

B5200 ▶

742 ⊙

SAGITTARIUS

B5200 ⊙

DMC FLOSS COLORS:

676   677

729   B5200

STITCH KEY:

♉	couching
⊗	cross stitch
✖	French knot(s)
▶	running stitch
◗	satin stitch
■	straight stitch

(see Stitch Guide beginning on page 12 for stitch instructions)

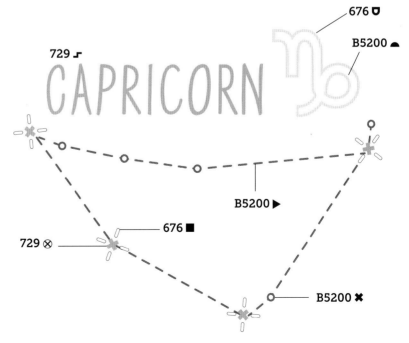

729 ⌐ CAPRICORN   **676** ♉   **B5200** ◗

B5200 ▶

729 ⊗   **676** ■

B5200 ✖

**DMC FLOSS
COLORS:**

B5200

STITCH KEY:

●	backstitch
✖	French knot(s)
★	star stitch
⌐	stem stitch

(see Stitch Guide
beginning on page 12
for stitch instructions)

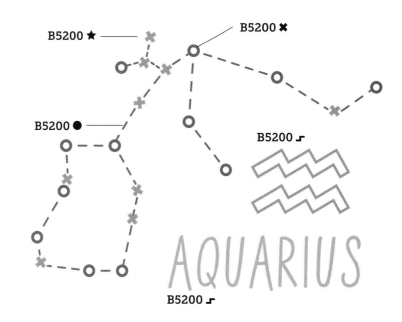

DMC FLOSS COLORS:

742   B5200

STITCH KEY:

O	chain stitch
⊗	cross stitch
✖	French knot(s)
▶	running stitch

(see Stitch Guide beginning on page 12 for stitch instructions)

B5200 ▶

742 O

B5200 O

PISCES

742 ⊗

B5200 ✖

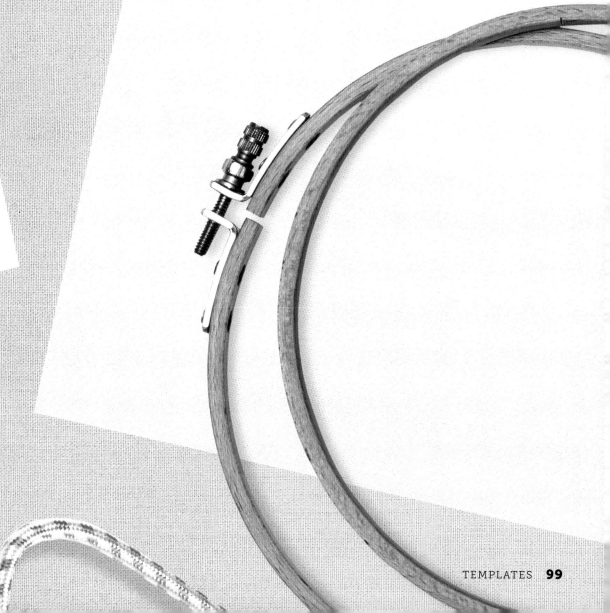

TEMPLATES

ARIES

pattern on page 27

Finished size : 6.1″ x 6.5″ (15.6 x 16.5 cm)

TAURUS

pattern on page 29

Finished size : 6.5″ x 6″ (16.7 x 15.4cm)

Finished size : 6.5" x 6.4" (16.6 x 16.2 cm)

CANCER

pattern on page 33

Finished size : 6.5" x 6.5" (16.5 x 16.5 cm)

Finished size : 6.5" x 6.2" (18.2 x 15.7 cm)

VIRGO

pattern on page 37

Finished size : 6.6" x 6.1" (16.7 x 15.6 cm)

Finished size : 6.5" x 6.4" (16.5 x 16.2 cm)

SCORPIO

pattern on page 41

Finished size : 6.5" x 6.5" (16.4 x 16.6 cm)

SAGITTARIUS

pattern on page 43

Finished size : 6.5" x 6.4" (16.5 x 16.3 cm)

CAPRICORN

pattern on page 45

Finished size : 6.3" x 6.5" (16 x 16.5 cm)

AQUARIUS

pattern on page 47

Finished size : 6.4" x 6.5" (16.2 x 16.5 cm)

PISCES
pattern on page 49

Finished size : 5.8″ x 6.5″ (14.8 x 16.4 cm)

MIDNIGHT BAT pattern on page 50

Finished size : 3.6" wide x 2.3" high (9.2 x 5.9 cm)

LUNA MOTH pattern on page 52

Finished size : 3.6" wide x 3.4" high (9.3 x 8.7 cm)

MOONLIGHT OWL pattern on page 54

Finished size : 4.2″ wide x 2.3″ high (10.7 x 5.8 cm)

PHASES OF THE MOON pattern on page 56

Finished size : 3.5″ wide x 3.4″ high (8.9 x 9.7 cm)

CRYSTALS pattern on page 58

Finished size : 3″ wide x 3.5″ high (7.4 x 8.8 cm)

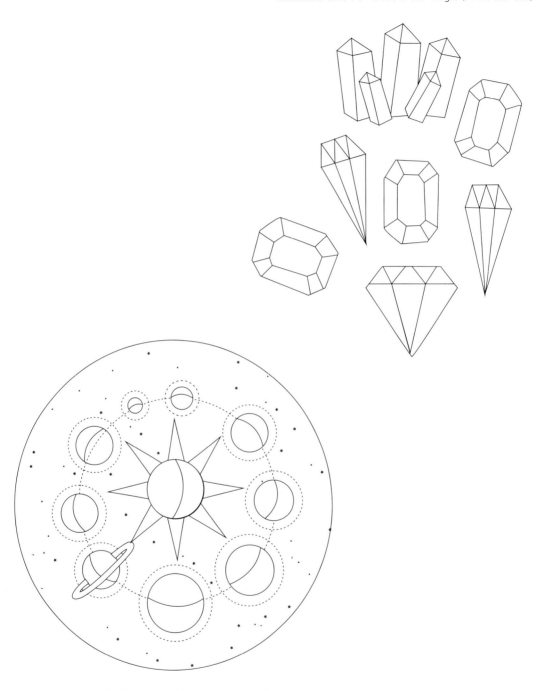

THE PLANETS pattern on page 60

Finished size : 3.4″ wide x 3.4″ high (8.8 x 8.8 cm)

TELESCOPE pattern on page 62

Finished size : 2.8″ wide x 2.5″ high (7.0 x 6.3 cm)

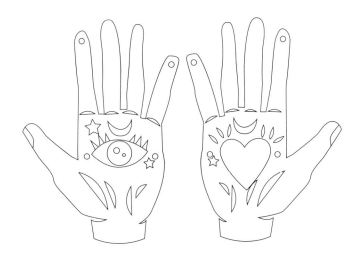

KNOWING HANDS pattern on page 64

Finished size : 3.4″ wide x 2.4″ high (8.7 x 6 cm)

TINY TOADSTOOLS pattern on page 66

Finished size : 3″ wide x 3.2″ high (7.7 x 8.1 cm)

THE SUN pattern on page 68

Finished size : 3.2″ wide x 3.2″ high (8.1 x 8 cm)

COMPASS pattern on page 70

Finished size : 3.3″ wide x 3.4″ high (8.5 x 8.7 cm)

LA LUNA pattern on page 74

Finished size : 3″ wide x 3″ high (7.7 x 7.7 cm)

BLACK CAT pattern on page 72

Finished size : 2.7" wide x 3" high (6.8 x 7.6 cm)

SUMMER FIREFLIES pattern on page 76

Finished size : 3.4" wide x 3" high (8.5 x 7.9 cm)

ARIES

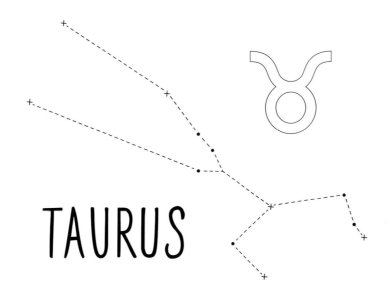

TAURUS

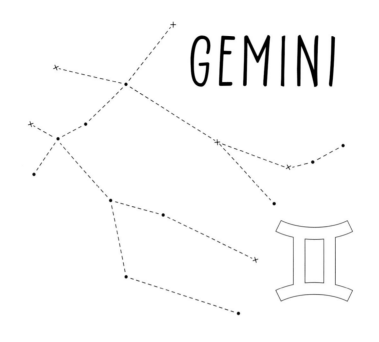

GEMINI

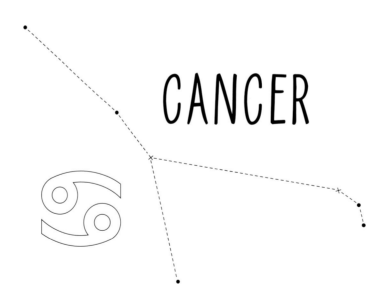

CANCER

LEO

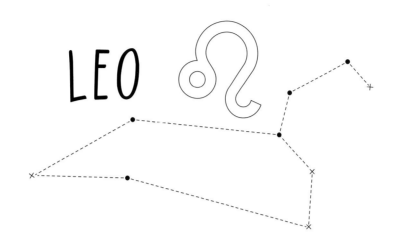

VIRGO

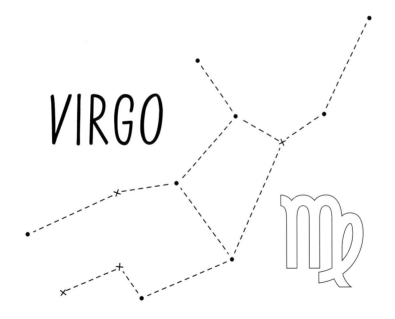

LIBRA

SCORPIO

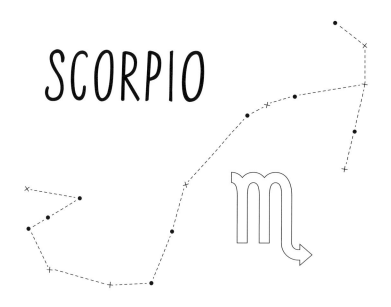

SAGITTARIUS

CAPRICORN

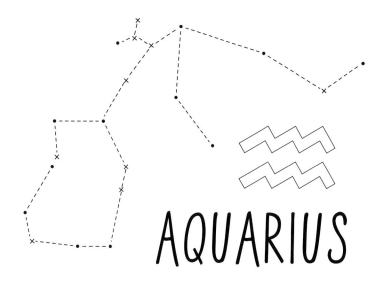

AQUARIUS

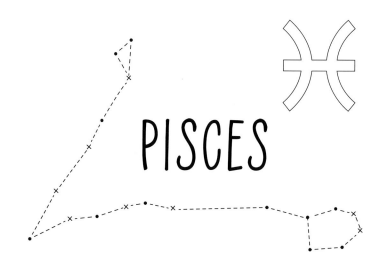

PISCES

ABOUT THE AUTHOR

Chilean illustrator and children's book author Maya Hanisch paints in colorful details that charm and enchant. Her amazing, folkloric-style illustrations give life to beautiful animals, stunning florals, all carefully embellished with tiny leaves, cute dots, and graceful embellishments with so much loveliness to discover.

Maya studied graphic design at Universidad Diego Portales in Santiago, Chile, and painting at the School of the Museum of Fine Arts in Boston, Massachusetts. Maya has taught classes and workshops at universities and book fairs around the world. Her paintings and collages have been exhibited both in Chile and abroad. Maya is the author of four books and this is the first time her art has been translated into embroidery.

ABOUT THE STITCHERS

EMILIE GANIERE is a born and raised midwesterner with a passion for creating. After spending her younger years as a traveling bard she has now settled into a pile of tea and embroidery supplies. You can find her lurking at local craft fairs, selling her wares on Etsy, and feeding table scraps to her local murder of crows.

ERICA INGRAM has a background with needlework as she has been cross stitching since age 11 but only in 2019 did she pick up embroidery. Embroidery has become an artistic outlet for Erica and she is happy to be able to share it with others!

ALLISON KOSTECKI is a California native currently living in Australia where she works as a fly-in fly-out COVID nurse for a remote outback mine site. She loves traveling, diving, skiing, and horseback riding. She's loves to take her embroidery on all of my travels and finds inspiration in nature she encounters.

DOMINIQUE MIYAKE is originally from Canada but have been living in Japan since 2004. Mother of three little ones, full-time editor and creator of English-learning materials, and owner of small embroidery business Three Houses Designs.

MEGAN POTTER is the servant to four cat gods who rule all her day time hours, but whenever they release her from her petting, playing and feeding obligations she's freed to spend her time indulging her passion for colour and her painterly sensibilities, blending her background as a watercolour painter into her embroidery and fiber arts pieces. Which is how she ends up spending most of her time stabbing things with needles, painting and playing cute farming sims on her Nintendo Switch. Find her, her cats and her art on Instagram at limitless.

ABBI SAWYER is an Air Force wife, dog mom currently living in California. Her mother taught her embroidery at a young age, and she has been working on improving it ever since. She spends her free time sewing dog bandanas and embroidering home decor for her shop, Calimo Design Co. Website: calimodesignco.com

GEMMA WINTER is an embroidery artist based in the Great Britain.